The Adventures of Scuba Jack

"Hi Artie," said Ozzie the Ostrich.
"What are you painting today?"
 "It's a picture of my grandmother Josephine,"
answered Artie. "I miss her so much."

Artie and Ozzie lived with other animals on a ranch and also traveled together in a petting zoo. There were turkeys, sheep, ducklings, and ponies.

ZOO

There were also piglets, cows, baby goats and
even a strutting peacock!
"It's hard when you lose a loved one," said Ozzie.

"When I paint her picture, I feel like I am close to her," said Artie. "It's like when we visit schools and children come and see us. They want to be near us, pet us and give us hugs. There's nothing better than to feel you are loved."

"When someone you love is gone, it is really hard. It makes you feel very sad," said Ozzie. "My grandfather was always ready for me to run to him and then he would give me hugs. I loved him very much. I try to remember my grandfather by giving myself a huge hug. It's like he is still here next to me."

Artie continued painting. It made him happy and sad at the same time. And that was okay. He was remembering his grandmother Josephine.

"Tomorrow we are going to visit children at a school," said Ozzie. "I think I'll rest up today and sit on that lovely bench over there by the flower garden."

Artie looked up from his painting. "I don't remember ever seeing that bench there before," he said. He set down his paints and walked over to join Ozzie at the bench.

"It's nice and shady here. I feel calm and relaxed", said Artie. "I remember my grandmother loved shady fields filled with flowers. She loved looking at the butterflies flit from flower to flower. She thought the butterflies were loved ones that passed away and came to visit. She would have loved sitting near this garden and smelling the beautiful flowers on the cool summer breeze.

"It's so peaceful," said Ozzie.
"I think I will paint her name across the front of the bench. Then I can sit here and think of her anytime I want."

Artie walked back to his paints and then brought them to the bench. He started with a beautiful purple J. Soon the bench had a lovely word painted on it. J O S E P H I N E.
When he was finished, he put his paints away. After the paint dried, he sat on the bench to admire his grandmother's name.

Josephine

"You did a great job, Artie," said Ozzie. "It's easy to see how much you loved her."

"I feel good when I sit here. I have many memories of her which help me feel better. When I begin to feel sad, I think about her and it puts a big smile on my face!" said Artie. "I think of her always and her kindness and love for me. She was the best!"

Artie looked over and noticed the flower garden had hundreds of colorful butterflies.

One butterfly landed right on Artie's nose. "Look how beautiful you are," Artie said to the butterfly. The butterfly danced on his nose, Artie laughed and said, " Are you my Grandmother Josephine? I miss you and love you so much!"

*This book is dedicated to my sister in law **Josephine Taormina**, who valiantly fought hard and bravely, against her battle with Leukemia. You are greatly missed and loved!*

Visit us at:

www.adventuresofscubajack.com